PLAYFUL POEMS

"Playful Poems"
By Seth and Tanika Warden
Illustrated by Kara Kniffen

Digital Layout by:
BDesign
www.bdesignstudiony.com

ISBN 978-0-615-87820-1

Pickle Pie Productions, LLC
PO Box 2424
Wilton, NY 12831
518-490-1118
picklepieproductions@yahoo.com

Printed in the U.S.A

How I wish Mosquito's ate burritos,
And sipped on Lemonade.

They would never get slapped, or even zapped,
If they could live this way.

We could play later at night, avoid a bite,
And never have to be sprayed.

How I wish Mosquito's ate burritos,
And sipped on Lemonade.

My nana is a ninja!
But you would never ever know.
Because she talks so quiet,
And she walks so slow.

She is gentle, she is kind,
And most certainly she is sweet.
But bad guys beware,
She will sweep you off your feet!

Nana the "NINJA"

If you have a healthy snack,
Do you think that you could share it?

Is it red, or is it orange?
Like an apple, or a carrot.

It might just be as nice
To have some beans and rice,
But fruit and veggies simply would be better.

If we have a healthy snack,
In each of our lunch sacks,
Maybe we could eat them all together!

A turtle named Terry, and a frog named Fred,
Swam through the swamp to a flower bed.

There were lots of silly lillies,
And the air was full of flies...

But neither of them could catch one,
No matter how hard they tried.

The Awesome ANTS

I saw a miniature mound,
Growing from the ground,
And from it came a thousand awesome ants.

They were lined all in a row,
And they put on quite a show,
as they danced their delicate little dance.

They gathered food for the queen,
Who is hardly ever seen,
And protect her from any sort of harm.

Everyone helps the best they can,
There's a thousand helping hands,
At the awesome ant farm!

Five little beans,
Were planted in a row.
No matter how much they were watered,
They just would not grow.

"Give them love and give them sun",
I heard my mommy tell me.
Then one day I realized...
Those beans were made of jelly!

Have you ever looked into the sky,
And wondered just how and why,
The clouds can form so many different shapes.

Some look like animals,
Some like cars,
Some look like a vine full of grapes.

Some seem to wave,
Some seem to cry,
Some seem to float on by.

Some go fast,
While others go slow,
Depending on how the wind will blow.

I saw a darling little duck, little duck.
Who had his feet stuck in the muck, in the muck.
Along came a rooster, who said "cluck, cluck, cluck!"
Just look at that little stuck duck!

I saw a shadow in my room,
Made from the bristles of a broom,
It was scary and it gave me quite a fright!

I knew just what it was,
But it scared me just because,
I flicked the switch and out went all the lights!

There are two important things
That every farmer knows;
You need the sun and the rain,
If you want your crops to grow!

Someday I hope to be,
As tall as the tallest tree.
So I could see all there is to see,
And be a home to the birds and bees.

My limbs would hold swings
For little boys and girls.
And I would grow food,
For all the silly squirrels.

I would change with the seasons,
In rain and in snow,
The sunshine gives me strength
So I can grow and grow.

Someday I hope to be,
As tall as the tallest tree.

Soaring in the moonlight,
Hearing every sound,
Searching for a friend,
Wondering "whoo, whoo" could be around?

My friends are all asleep
But I am ready for a flight!
I wish they slept during the day like me,
And would wake up with the night.

With the stars in her eyes,
And feathers on her feet,
She sat patiently perched,
Waiting for something to eat.

"LONLEY" the owl

I tried to say hello,
But my mouth was full of jello,
And it ended in quite a mighty mess.

It was all over the floor,
Now I'll have to get some more,
but first I have to wash it off my dress!

Herbert loves sherbert,
And he eats it every night.

His eyes will squeeze,
His brain will freeze,
As he takes too big a bite.

It only takes a second,
For soon the pain will ease.
So Herbert eat your sherbert,
A little slower won't you please?

Animals are everywhere!
On the ground and in the air!
On the sand and in the sea,
Some animals look just like me!

Animals make sounds,
That you'll hear all around,
In the woods or even at a zoo.
There are some animals around,
Who can even make a sound
That sounds like me and you!

I love all kinds of animals
In case you couldn't tell,
Even ones that don't have fun,
And the ones that really smell!

As the stars sparkle in the night time sky,
So does the love that I see in your eyes.
It brings me hope, peace and deep inside,
I will forever be standing by your side.

Pickle Pie Productions, llc

Offering quality educational children's music and literature.

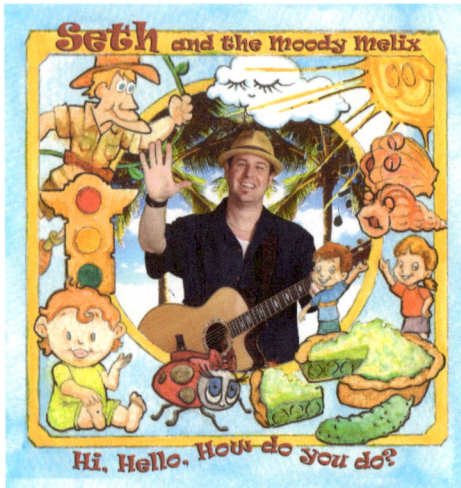

Hi, Hello, How do you do?
by Seth and the Moody Melix
Childrens music CD

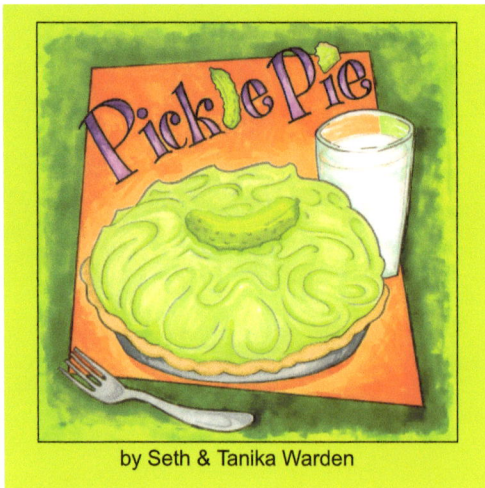

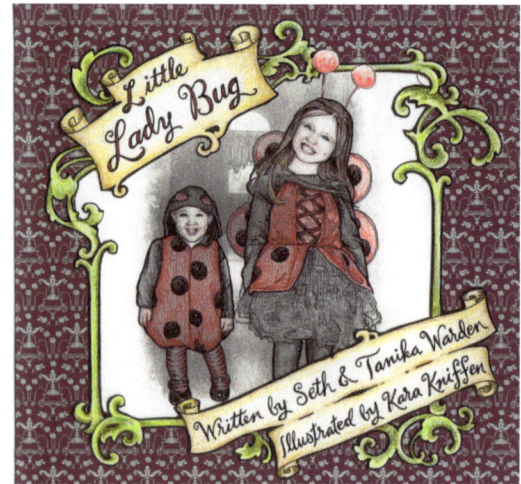

Pickle Pie
Children's Book
Extra features include Recipe and Sheet music

Little Lady Bug
Children's Book
Extra features include Sheet music